APA
Simplified

Your Concise Guide
to the 7th Edition

Mark Hatala, Ph.D.

Greentop Academic Press • Greentop, Missouri

APA Simplified: Your concise guide to the 7th edition
by Mark Hatala, Ph.D.

ISBN-13: 978-1-933167-54-1
ISBN-10: 1-933167-54-8

Book Design: Charles Dunbar

The font used in this book is Times New Roman, which is an approved font of the American Psychological Association; however, the interior uses a 10-point font to save space - APA style requires a 12-point font.

To incorporate this book into your classroom, visit our website at APAcentral.com

Table of Contents

Why this book

Why this book

Although I have written several books on APA style, this is my first "short" book on the subject. So why now? A couple of reasons.

First, the *Publication Manual* has come out in a new 7th edition, and a number of changes have been made to the way academic writing is presented, cited, and referenced. So the timing is right.

Second, while the APA publishes its own "concise" guide to APA style for students, it is 326 pages long! That is NOT concise, in my opinion, especially since the full-blown *Publication Manual* is 427 pages. Concise is 50 pages or less, not 100 pages shorter than the full guide that covers every possible contingency in writing. Also, the APA guides use the EXACT SAME examples in both books, which I find unhelpful.

Third, most other "brief" guides are all about formatting, not writing. A two-minute YouTube video can teach you all you need to know about formatting, but it takes a book to teach you how to write an APA style paper.

Finally, I think that the other "brief" guides on the market are outdated. They often have instructions on how to format your paper using Microsoft Word (as if we live in 1998) and their "sample papers" are on non-academic topics like Oprah Winfrey (and that's not a misprint). They also provide no instruction on how to actually FIND academic research.

Therefore, this book will guide you through the 7th edition of the APA style *Publication Manual* in a way that is brief, concise, and relevant to papers written in the 2020s (and beyond).

In addition to my other books (which go into greater detail), I have a number of videos explaining APA style on both YouTube and my website, APAcentral.com. The website brings together videos, supplements, worksheets, reference lists, and just about anything else you would need to write a successful APA style paper, which is why I say that all of my writing is "powered by APA Central." So check it out.

You made the right (or "write") choice in buying this book.

Mark Hatala, Ph.D.
Professor of Psychology
Truman State University

Finding appropriate research

You have your topic - now what? First of all, congratulations! If you also have a working title for your paper, it's pretty much halfway written at this point. However, now you need to find appropriate academic research on your topic, and that search is going to start on the web.

Wikipedia

While using *Wikipedia* as a reference in your paper tells your professor "I didn't try, and I don't care," specific research topics are based on cited research, and the citations are referenced at the bottom of the *Wikipedia* webpage. For example, a broad topic like PTSD (Post Traumatic Stress Disorder) has 267 (!) research articles cited on *Wikipedia*, and these articles are literally a click away from being incorporated into a research paper. Even a narrow topic like "mnemonics" has 29 cited research articles.

Psychology databases - PsychINFO and PsychARTICLES

PsycINFO and PsychARTICLES are available through academic libraries and are both published by the American Psychological Association (otherwise known as the APA), although they differ in the level of access they provide. PsycINFO searches much more broadly (literally millions of articles, dissertations, theses, papers, etc.), but often only provides the abstract (or summary) of an article. PsychARTICLES provides full text for articles which are published by the APA, but only searches the 90 journals that are part of this database. Since both PsycINFO and PsychARTICLES are published by the APA, all of the information in PsychARTICLES is redundant with PsychINFO, which means that anything that can be found in PsychARTICLES will also be found (including the full-text component) in PsychINFO.

Google and Google Scholar

Google Scholar (scholar.google.com) is an even broader database than PsycINFO and PsychARTICLES, and includes cross-disciplinary research that might not appear in the psychology databases. Google Scholar (and just plain old Google.com) also contains links to websites, and many times information from a website is the most up-to-date source for a particular topic. Information from sources like the Mayo Clinic (mayoclinic. org) and the Centers for Disease Control and Prevention (cdc.gov) are credible and cover a variety of scientific topics.

Data mining from research articles and textbooks

The truth is that someone with a Ph.D. has already done your literature search for you - the people who write research articles and textbooks. Authors of academic works cite the research that is relevant to their topic, and these are easily found in the reference section of a research paper or a textbook. This method is a gift that keeps on giving because it creates a positive feedback loop of published researchers doing your work for you. It frees you from having to determine whether an article is "important" or not, and it provides a wide range of relevant research articles to choose from. Your professor will know what research is important, and by using this method to find articles, you won't be

8

blindsided by them asking "Why didn't you use the most famous article on this topic in your paper?!"

The bottom line

I believe that incorporating all of the above methods is the best and most exhaustive way of finding appropriate research on your topic. Use *Wikipedia* to help find a topic that is interesting to you, then find more relevant articles using the full-text feature available through the psychology databases. Next, find a general textbook (or even better, a more specific textbook that covers your topic) and see what foundational research they cite. Finally, use Google Scholar to find the most up-to-date web-based information. In this way, all of your bases are covered - you'll have a variety of sources for your topic, from the foundational work to the most recent research on your topic.

Writing your paper

Now that you have collected and read all of your articles, you are ready to start writing! Academic papers tend to be very "dry" and to the point - just the facts - with little need to entertain the reader. APA style papers can seem "formulaic" and that is appropriate, because you are essentially writing according to a formula. The same kinds of things are expected in all academic papers - a review of the literature, citation of research, references, etc. Departing from the formula does not make you creative so much as it makes you **wrong**. This is not to say that writing to a formula is easy. It is, however, very straightforward.

Here is a point that I cannot stress enough - write from an outline! The time it takes to write an outline is more than made up in the time it saves you when it comes time to write your paper. Both student and "professional" (meaning a paper submitted for publication) APA style papers follow a basic structure. Student papers are introduction, body, and conclusion. Since professional papers contain original research, they also have specific sections devoted to methodology and statistical results. The "shape" of both types of manuscripts are the same - like an hourglass - broad at the beginning, narrow in the middle, and broad at the end. In other words, your paper should begin and end in fairly broad generalities, and discuss specific research in the middle.

Opening paragraph

So how should you begin? I tell my students to always start their paper by just plugging in the phrase: "People have always wondered about [insert topic] and how it influences them and changes their lives." The introduction can pretty much go anywhere after that! I don't want students to actually USE that phrase, but it acts as a placeholder in their mind of how the paper should begin. And see, they've already started writing! Begin with a universal "hook" to engage the reader, and then get into the research.

The thesis statement provides a concise summary of what the paper is going to be about, and it appears as the last sentence of the introduction. The thesis statement is important because it informs the reader about the organization of the rest of the paper. In a student paper, the body of the paper will unfold from the thesis. In a professional paper, the "thesis" is usually encompassed in a "Purpose of the Present Study" section that, while more detailed and specific (because it's about THEIR study), serves the exact same purpose as a thesis statement.

The relevant literature on your topic

Once you have your opening paragraph, the rest of your paper writes itself. Well, almost. The body of your paper, to go back to the hourglass analogy, is where your paper begins to get specific and you talk about individual research studies. How much should you talk about each study? Well, here the APA style manual becomes oddly specific. While discouraging single-sentence paragraphs, the ideal is to write paragraphs of three to five sentences without going over one typed page.

But how do you get to that point? In a student paper, try to identify three "themes" or "commonalities" to guide your writing. The "themes" will vary from paper to paper based on the topic you choose and the research which is available, but there are a number of common themes which work across a variety of papers. For example, many conditions have multiple treatments which are available, so you might examine each of these in a different paragraph. This is effective in that it also allows you to "compare and contrast" the different treatments. The paper writes itself.

Many topics in clinical psychology can follow a "definition, causes, symptoms, and treatments" format. Whether you are writing about agoraphobia, body dysmorphic disorder, obsessive-compulsive disorder (OCD), or trichotillomania (TTM), you can have a paragraph which defines the disorder, followed by one which discusses the causes (if they are known, but this can be speculation too), followed by one on the symptoms, and then one on the treatment (or treatments) available.

Although my examples are from psychology, the number of topics you might choose to write about using APA style is pretty much infinite, so the number of "themes" is even *more* infinite (if such a thing is possible). Oftentimes the themes which you identify will be something subject specific, such as a comparison of different approaches to the same topic (like early child education), or ways of measuring the topic of interest (like parenting). Don't be afraid to go where the research takes you - the "themes" discussed above are just ones which are the easiest to identify.

In a professional paper, the literature review follows the hypotheses stated in the "Purpose of the Present Study" section. Basically, you're writing about the research that supports your hypotheses, and how the methodology used in those studies is relevant to the design of your own study.

Methods and Results

These sections are only going to appear in a professional paper where you actually perform a research study.

The **Methods** section provides information about how the data was collected, how participants were selected, the research design, and how the study was actually conducted. This information is important because it will allow other researchers to replicate the study.

The **Results** section is a summary of the statistical results of your study. The specific values obtained from statistical tests (such as t tests, F ratios, etc.) are presented in this section, along with supplementary information about effect sizes, confidence intervals, and the probability of obtaining those results (the p values).

The Conclusion or Discussion

The final part of your paper, logically enough, is the conclusion (or **Discussion**, if it's a professional paper). So how should your paper end? Remembering our hourglass analogy, the paper ends by broadening the discussion back to how the topic is related to the future of humanity or otherwise improves the human condition.

An ideal thing to discuss in the conclusion are future areas of research, because nothing shows greater insight than making intelligent suggestions about where you see future research on a particular topic heading. Suggestions for future research are also a subtle way to insert your own thoughts and opinions about the research into your paper.

Citations

Citations get their own section because of the many problems they cause. It seems easy enough - you should use a citation in your paper whenever you are paraphrasing, discussing someone else's ideas, or taking a direct quote from another manuscript. **Basically, it should be clear, when you're writing about someone else's research, whose research it is that you're writing about.** If you're writing about your own thoughts, you don't need a citation. When you start writing about someone else's, you need to give them attribution or credit.

The way sources are cited in APA style depends on how many authors there are. When there are one or two, citation is simple because you just list everyone every time the source is cited. When there are three or more authors, things are slightly more complicated - you have to list the first author followed by "et al." - but still pretty simple! When sources are from a "group author" things get even *more* complicated, so I included a special section on that!

Citations can occur in the text of a sentence (a narrative citation) or parenthetically (a parenthetical citation), and I will provide examples of how each would be used with the same source material. To keep things congruent, all the sources deal with the topic of conformity.

Source with one author

When a source has one author, the last name of the author should be provided every time the source is cited, whether it is an initial or subsequent citation, and regardless of whether the citation is narrative or parenthetical. For example:

Source

Pasupathi, M. (1999). Age differences in response to conformity pressure for emotional
and nonemotional material. *Psychology and Aging, 14*(1), 170-174.
http://doi.org/dnftfh

Narrative format
Pasupathi (1999) found that . . .

Parenthetical format
. . . however, others (Pasupathi, 1999) have found that . . .

Source with two authors

When a source has two authors, BOTH authors should be provided every time the source is cited, regardless of whether it is an initial or subsequent citation, and regardless of whether the citation is narrative or parenthetical. The only difference is that since there are now two authors, you need to include "and" between the authors names for a narrative citation, and an ampersand ("&") between the authors names for a parenthetical citation. For example:

Source
Santee, R. T. & Jackson, S. E. (1982). Identity implications of conformity: Sex differences in normative and attributional judgments. *Social Psychology Quarterly*, *45*(2), 121-125. https://doi.org/10.2307/3033935

Narrative format
Santee and Jackson (1982) found that . . .

Parenthetical format
. . . however, others (Santee & Jackson, 1982) have found that . . .

Source with three or more authors

Citation simplifies again when a source has three or more authors, because you just need to provide the last name of the first author followed by "et al." whenever the work appears in your paper. For an example of a source with three authors:

Source
Stowell, J. R., Oldham, T., & Bennett, D. (2010). Using student response systems ("clickers") to combat conformity and shyness. *Teaching of Psychology*, *37*(2), 135-140. http://doi.org/cr9bjx

Narrative format
Stowell et al. (2010) found that . . .

Parenthetical format
. . . however, others (Stowell et al., 2010) have found that . . .

Source with a group author (that can be abbreviated)

Citation becomes a little more complicated when using a source with group authors, mostly because when the "group authors" can be abbreviated, this causes a difference in the formatting of initial and subsequent citations. For example, maybe you're working on a paper on health risks and outcomes and want to provide information on the social determinants of health (SDOH) in the United States. It turns out that the Centers for Disease Control and Prevention have a web page dedicated to that exact topic!

So far, so good! However, the Centers for Disease Control and Prevention is abbreviated as CDC (who knows where the "P" goes, but I think there's a joke there), so when cited as a source in a paper, things change from the initial to subsequent citations. For example, here is the source reference:

Source
Centers for Disease Control and Prevention. (2018, January 29). *Social determinants of health: Know what affects health.* https://www.cdc.gov/socialdeterminants/ index.htm

This is the exact page on the CDC's website where this material appears. It includes a date, which identifies the most recent edit, on January 29th, 2018 - the source which will be cited. Since there is no individual author for the page, the "group author" (Centers for Disease Control and Prevention) is provided.

Here's where things get complicated. The "group author" name should be provided the first time the source is cited, but if the group author name can be abbreviated, subsequent citations should just be the abbreviation. For our example on health risks, it would appear as:

Narrative format
1st citation - The Centers for Disease Control and Prevention (CDC, 2018) found that . . .
Subsequent citation - The CDC (2018) found that . . .

Parenthetical format
1st citation - . . . however, others (Centers for Disease Control and Prevention [CDC], 2018) have found that . . .
Subsequent citation - . . . however, others (CDC, 2018) have found that . . .

Please note the brackets around "CDC" in the initial parenthetical citation of this source. Can it be complicated to use a group author as a source? Yes! But is there a logic behind how to reference and cite such a source? Yes.

References

The way sources are referenced in APA style depends on whether they are a **textual work** (which includes journal articles, books, book chapters, etc.), **audiovisual media** (podcasts, YouTube videos, you name it), **online media** (websites, tweets, and social media) or just about anything else (primarily data sets and software). All references contain the same information: the author (or authors), the year of publication, the title of the work, and information about where it was published (so that the reader can retrieve it).

References - Textual Works

Research journals

The majority of sources in an academic paper should be work published in peer-reviewed research journals. A generic example of a journal reference would be pretty meaningless, so here's an actual one, and then a breakdown of the component parts:

Lee, A. Y. (2002). Effects of implicit memory on memory-based versus stimulus-based brand choice. *Journal of Marketing Research, 39*(4), 440-454. http://doi.org/c4j8zv

So, to deconstruct the reference, it takes the following form:

First author last name, First author first name initial. First author middle name initial. (#### year of publication). Title of the journal article. *Name of the Periodical,* ## *volume number of periodical*(#issue number of periodical - if available), ### page numbers of article. http://doi.org/######## - if available

All the information to find the reference is there: author, year, title, and publication information. To point out a few things though, you might notice that the name and volume number of the periodical is in italics. If there is an issue number for the periodical, it is put in parentheses right next to the volume number, so there is no space between them.

The number of authors in a reference

You include up to 20 authors in a reference, BUT if there are over 20 authors, the first 19 are listed, then an ellipses, and then the last author. I've never actually seen a source with over 20 authors, and can only imagine what a meeting to determine authorship with 20 authors would be like.

What are DOI numbers?

DOI (digital object identifier) numbers identify where a particular source is "permanently" stored in a digital network, and have become standard for periodicals (less so for books) since they were introduced in 2000. DOI numbers are presented at the end of a reference as a hyperlink, meaning that they have the whole http://doi.org . . . set-up. This is so that the reader can find the reference by literally pasting the link into their browser. According to the 7th edition you can use either the underlined "blue" default for a hyperlink in your paper, or you can write the DOI link as plain text. Just try to be consistent! I've chosen to use plain text throughout this book so that I don't have to pay extra for two-color printing!

What do you do if you find a journal article without an assigned DOI? You leave it off the reference. Really, if there's no assigned DOI, what else can you do?

Shortening DOI numbers

Why do DOI numbers have to be so long?! Why isn't there a service to shorten them? Well, there is! Just go to the website provided by the International DOI Foundation (http://shortdoi.org) and plug the long DOI into their "shortener." For example, the Lee (2002) article's assigned DOI is http://dx.doi.org/10.1509/jmkr.39.4.440.19119 and it's "shortened" DOI is http://doi.org/c4j8zv. I have tried to use the shortened DOIs throughout this book, but the *Publication Manual* says that you don't need to remain consistent in your paper on this matter.

Books

Books are a useful source of information when you're writing a paper. As with research journals, a generic example of a book reference is a little silly without context, so here's an actual book reference, and then a breakdown:

Plunkett, J. M. (2011). *Bipolar disorder: Causes, diagnosis and treatment.* Nova Science Publishers.

Taking the reference apart, it looks like:

First author last name, First author first name initial. First author middle name initial. (#### year the book was published). *Title of the book.* Name of the publisher.

Books don't usually have a DOI number assigned to them, but if you find one that does, just put it at the end of the reference, the same way you would for a journal article.

Book chapters

Book chapters are treated as a hybrid of a book and a journal because books, like journals, have editors. Journals have editors too, but they're not listed in the references. Why? Who knows? Again, it's unclear, so here's an example:

Foa, E. B., & Franklin, M. E. (2001). Obsessive-compulsive disorder. In D. H. Barlow (Ed.), *Clinical handbook of psychological disorders: A step-by-step treatment manual* (3rd ed., pp. 209-263). The Guilford Press.

All of the references contain different combinations of the same information, but there are a few unique aspects of book chapters that I want to make note of. For example, you might notice that where the author of the chapter is listed last name first, the editors are listed last name last, which switches things up. The names of the editors are also followed by either "(Ed.)" or "(Eds.)" depending on how many of them there are. Similar to a journal article, you list the page numbers of the chapter, but unlike a journal article, you precede this with "pp." (if there are multiple pages).

Magazine article - In print or online

You might decide to use a magazine article to provide some "pop culture" or "edgy" material to your introduction. My recommendation would be to use this source material very sparingly. With that warning in mind, here is how you would reference a magazine article, in this case an article about the cultural importance of the television show *Sex and the City*.

In print:

Armstrong, J. K. (2018, May 11). Sex and the City and us: How four single women changed the way we think, live, and love. *Entertainment Weekly, 1514*, 32-35.

Online:

Armstrong, J. K. (2018, May 5). Sex and the City and us: How four single women changed the way we think, live, and love. *Entertainment Weekly*. http://www.ew.com/ article/2018/05/05/sex-and-the-city-and-us

You may notice that the dates are different on the "in print" and "online" editions of the same article. Both are actually correct, and my guess is that for *Entertainment Weekly*, information appears on their website before it appears in print. Or who knows? Print media is dead anyway.

Additionally, if you just wanted to cite the book itself rather than a magazine article about it, the book reference would look like this:

Armstrong, J. K. (2018). *Sex and the City and us: How four single women changed the way we think, live, and love.* Simon & Schuster.

Newspaper article - in print or online

Newspapers can be a more up-to-date source for a particular topic. Although I feel some trepidation in encouraging the use of newspapers as sources in academic papers, here is how a reference looks for a newspaper article on agoraphobia:

In print:

Lukits, A. (2016, September 19). Fear of open spaces may be linked to animal instincts. *The Wall Street Journal*, D4.

Note: "D4" refers to the page number the article appeared on in the physical newspaper.

Online:

Lukits, A. (2016, September 19). Fear of open spaces may be linked to animal instincts. *The Wall Street Journal*. https://www.wsj.com/articles/fear-of-open-spaces-may-be-linked-to-animal-instincts-1474290002

Dictionary

For general spelling, APA style uses the *Meriam-Webster.com Dictionary*; therefore, so should you, but only if it is absolutely necessary! A number of very poor student papers include the phrase *"Webster's* defines _____ as _____."* as if they were giving a speech and believe a dictionary is an appropriate source for a college paper. With that said, here is how you would reference a dictionary entry for the word "memory" (if you REALLY had to):

Merriam-Webster. (n.d.). Memory. In *Merriam-Webster.com dictionary*. Retrieved June
12, 2018, from http://merriam-webster.com/dictionary/memory

Note: Since this dictionary is constantly updated and previous versions are not archived (see the *Wikipedia* discussion below), you should use "n.d." (for "no date") as the publication year, and include a retrieval date.

Wikipedia

Have you heard of *Wikipedia*? If you haven't, you should check it out! *Wikipedia* is a good example that we are all familiar with to tease apart the issues with citing and referencing a "textual" source found online. One would think that *Wikipedia* would be considered to be "online media" by the criteria set by the *Publication Manual* because "online" is the only way to retrieve it, but one would be WRONG! It turns out that *Wikipedia*, although it is only accessible online, is considered to be a "textual work" because it is like an encyclopedia, and encyclopedias are "textual works." Forget about the whole "online" and "website" thing. Also, forget that *Wikipedia* is constantly edited and updated (online), so entries can change from day to day. There are archived and "stable" *Wikipedia* pages for a particular topic, even if they are only "stable" for a few moments. Since I believe that you should never actually use *Wikipedia* as a source for your paper, this section is something of a moot point, but let's continue!

Ironically, *Wikipedia* has an entry for "APA style." Let's use it in our example!

How would we cite and reference a *Wikipedia* entry? Since *Wikipedia* is "editable" and always changing, we would provide the date that WE accessed the website. So, a narrative citation might look something like:

According to "APA style" (2019), researchers have been given guidance on how to format academic papers.

And a parenthetical citation would look like:

Researchers have been given guidance on how to format academic papers ("APA style," 2019).

Now for the reference! Since *Wikipedia* is archived and "stable," we need to provide both a retrieval date and a link to the page we used, so theoretically, someone could see what the *Wikipedia* entry for "APA style" was from that particular day in the past. Would that actually ever happen? Seems unlikely. But again, APA style doesn't have to make sense, we just have to do what it says. Using the date that I'm writing this (in Belgrade, Serbia, of all places), the reference would look like:

APA style. (2019, June 27). In *Wikipedia*. http://en.wikipedia.org/wiki/APA_style

All of the information is there. Since there is no "author" we just put the topic, the date is the day we accessed it, we got the information from *Wikipedia* (which is in italics, because it's a type of encyclopedia), and we provide a link to the web page. It's just that easy!

The *DSM-5* as an alternative to dictionaries and encyclopedias

You might be asking yourself what to do if you're writing a paper and just can't find the definition of a term or clinical diagnosis. Rather than turn to a dictionary or encyclopedia, I would recommend using the latest edition of the *Diagnostic and Statistical Manual of Mental Disorders*, which is published by the American Psychiatric Association. We're now in the fifth edition of the book, which is why it is known in psychology as the *DSM-5*. It's not easy material to get through, and reading about symptoms and diagnoses might cause you to begin diagnosing yourself, your roommate, and members of your family with many disorders that they don't have. But, if you're looking for a definition of PTSD, OCD, SAD, or just about anything else in clinical psychology, here is your source:

American Psychiatric Association. (2013). *Diagnostic and statistical manual of mental disorders* (5th ed.). http://doi.org/brfw

Note: The *DSM-5* also has an assigned DOI number, and I have put the "shortened" version in the reference, as the "long" version is: http://doi.org/10.1176/appi.books.9780890425596

Blog post

I find it interesting that even though blogs only appear online ("blog" derives from "web log"), APA style considers them to be a "textual work" rather than "online media."

The reference does not need to be identified as a blog post, and the "publisher" is in italics (like a research journal!), followed by the URL.

Serdar, K. L. (2014, July 16). Female body image and the mass media: Perspectives on how women internalize the ideal beauty standard. *The Myriad*. http://d-muntyan1215-dc.blogspot.com/2014/07/female-body-image-and-mass-media

Press release

Press releases can be good because they present the most up-to-date information available. The problem is that if you're citing a press release from several years ago, the material might already be dated, or incorrect. The APA website featuring this press release explicitly states that a press release might contain "outdated science or missing details" by the time it is accessed. So, unless the press release has been issued within the past year, I would avoid including it in your paper, but I'm going to violate that rule in the example:

American Psychological Association. (2010, August 13). *Memory researchers explain latest findings on improving the mind, stopping memory loss* [Press release]. http://www.apa.org/news/press/releases/2010/08/memory-loss

Doctoral dissertations and master's theses
These are sources that you are unlikely to use in your paper, but you may run across them while conducting a search of online psychology databases. Doctoral dissertations and master's theses are identified as such (in brackets) after the title of the work (which is italicized). Unpublished doctoral dissertations are usually "unpublished" for a reason, and so you probably won't use them as a source.

Hatala, M. N. (1993). *A test of the additive unique-features model using consumer product preferences* [Unpublished doctoral dissertation]. Ohio University.

Note: This is my actual dissertation and it has a $20 bill taped to the title page. The last time I visited it in Ohio University's Alden Library (in 2004), the $20 was still there.

References - Audiovisual Media
Lots of great information can be gleaned from YouTube, TED Talks, or podcasts (or in the next section, Twitter or Facebook), and APA style teaches how to reference it!

YouTube
The title of a YouTube video is italicized in a reference, and whoever uploaded the video is considered to be the "author." The "date" is when it was uploaded.
In the spirit of self-promotion, here is one of my YouTube videos on the changes to the APA style manual from the 6th to 7th edition with a discussion group of college students:

Hatala, M. [Hatala Testing]. (2019, November 18). *Top 10 changes in the APA style manual - 6th to 7th edition* [Video]. YouTube. https://www.youtube.com/watch??v=YDp9T4eCOJM

The *Publication Manual* provides guidance if you wanted to provide a direct quote of some of my wisdom from this video. It would include a "time stamp" for the beginning of the quotation, and would look like this:

In earlier editions of APA style there was "a difference between the initial and subsequent citation" (Hatala, 2019, 7:43) of sources within a manuscript.

TED Talks
The interesting thing about TED Talks (although there are MANY interesting things about them) is that they are cited and referenced differently based on whether they are watched on YouTube or the TED website (although they might appear on both)!
Confused? Me too! For example, social psychologist Amy Cuddy has a very

interesting TED Talk on body language and how it impacts how people view us, as well as how we view ourselves. If you watch it on YouTube, then TED is credited as the author, a parenthetical citation would look like "(TED, 2012)" and the reference looks like:

TED. (2012, October 1). *Amy Cuddy: Your body language may shape who you are* [Video]. YouTube. https://www.youtube.com/watch?v=Ks-_Mh1QhMc&t=328s

However, if the exact same video is viewed on the TED website, you would credit Cuddy as the author, a parenthetical citation would look like "(Cuddy, 2012)" and the reference would look like:

Cuddy, A. (2012, June). *Your body language may shape who you are* [Video]. TED Conferences. https://www.ted.com/talks/amy_cuddy_your_body_language_may_shape_who_you_are?language=en

Why?! I'm unwilling to try to explain the logic here, because I don't understand it either, but I think it follows the same logic as making a blog post a "textual work" rather than "online media."

Television show - individual episode
I'm a huge fan of *Arrested Development*, and this is one of the best episodes, where the characters try to find a guy named "Hermano" because they don't realize that it is Spanish for "brother." Why would you include an episode of *Arrested Development* in your paper? Good question! However, the reference contains information about the writers, director, original airdate, title, season and episode number, producers, the title of the series, and the production companies involved in making the episode. A narrative citation would include the writers (so, "Hurwitz et al. (2004)") and a parenthetical citation the same thing ("(Hurwitz et al., 2004)"), except in parentheses.

Hurwitz, M., Rosenstock, R., & Martin, C. (Writers), & Chandrasekhar, J. (Director). (2004, February 15). Beef consomme (Season 1, Episode 13) [Television series episode]. In M. Hurwitz (Executive producer), *Arrested Development*. Imagine Television; The Hurwitz Company; Twentieth Century Fox Television.

Podcast
Like for many people, podcasts have replaced radio in my life. I still haven't had occasion to reference a podcast, but if you had to, this is how you would do it:

Carlson, B., & Batnick, M. (Hosts). (2020, January 15). The 10 best jobs in America (No. 121) [Audio podcast episode]. In *Animal Spirits*. https://awealthof commonsense.com/2020/01/animal-spirits-the-10-best-jobs-in-america/

Note: This is a podcast about personal finance that I like quite a bit.

Music album and music video

Vampire Weekend. (2019). This Life [Song]. On *Father of the bride*. Columbia.

Now you can judge me on my taste in music, but I need an example, so I'm going to use something that I like. The group is considered to be the "author" if you need to make a citation ("Vampire Weekend (2019)" in a narrative citation, for example). If you want to know what Ezra Koenig is going to look like in 30 years, flip to the back cover and take a look at my picture. If you wanted to cite the music video of the song, it would be referenced as follows:

Vampire Weekend. (2019, May 20). *Vampire Weekend - This Life* [Video]. YouTube. https://www.youtube.com/watch?v=FwkrrU2WYKg

Film

Forman, M. (Director). (1984). *Amadeus* [Film]. Orion Pictures.

I'm a big fan of Mozart, so his biopic gets to be the "film" example. The director is credited as the "author," and so is listed in a narrative or parenthetical citation.

References - Online media
Online media has deserved a dedicated section of APA style coverage, and with the 7th edition, finally receives one. The *Publication Manual* breaks "online media" into social media and websites, so I will discuss each of them in turn.

Social media

Twitter
I value my sanity, so I stay off Twitter, but famous people have been known to tweet important information. You should retain the spelling and capitalization in a tweet, and reproduce any emojis (if possible). In order to avoid any political issues, here is an innocuous tweet from Barack Obama wishing his wife Michelle a happy birthday:

Obama, B. [@BarackObama] (2020, January 15). *In every scene, you are my star, @MichelleObama! Happy birthday baby!* [Image attached] [Tweet]. Twitter. https://twitter.com/BarackObama/status/1218174463046553600

Note: If you wanted to make a parenthetical citation of this tweet, it would look like: (Obama, 2020)

Facebook post
Social media posts are interesting because it makes a difference whether someone's account is "public" or not. If a Facebook post can only be accessed by someone

who is a "friend," then it is classified as a "personal communication," which means that it's like a letter, phone conversation, or an email. Personal communications don't require a reference, just a citation. If a Facebook account is "public" (like celebrities, politicians, and public figures), then both a reference and citation are required.

In keeping with non-political examples from famous people, here is a Facebook post from Barack Obama about MLK Day. His account is public, so anyone can see his posts. Here is how the post would be referenced (note that it gets cut off after the first 20 words, so you don't need to write the entire post):

Obama, B. (2020, January 20). *Every so often, I re-read Dr. King's Letter from a Birmingham Jail. While some of the injustices may have changed* [Image attached] [Status update]. Facebook. https://www.facebook.com/barackobama/posts/10157369262941749

Note: An appropriate question to ask when using a Facebook status update in an academic paper would be, "Why am I using a Facebook status update in an academic paper? What am I THINKING?!" Great question! Really, it's a mystery.

Further note: This format should also be used for other social media sites which, in my opinion, should never appear in an academic paper, like LinkedIn, Tumblr, etc.

Instagram photo

Why might someone use Instagram as a source? Because there ARE unique things to access via social media! For example, Phillip Zimbardo occasionally posts archival photos from his (in)famous Stanford Prison Experiment, such as the newspaper ad used to recruit student participants. As with tweets, Facebook updates, etc, this outlet should be used VERY sparingly. Here is his post for winning the APA's Gold Medal Award:

Phillip Zimbardo [@phillip_zimbardo]. (2015, November 17). *Phil Zimbardo has been chosen to receive the APA's Gold Medal Award for Lifetime Achievement in the Science of Psychology* [Photograph]. Instagram. https://www.instagram.com/p/-M4HeaBoxc/

Websites and web pages

The *Publication Manual* points out that the term "website" can cause confusion because it is so all-encompassing. For example, although most journal articles are available online, they are considered to be "textual works" for purposes of reference. So what is "online media?" **Basically, a source is classified as "online media" if that is the only way to retrieve it**. You might then ask why *Wikipedia* and blogs are considered to be "textual works" when they're only found online? Well, according to the *Publication Manual*, if a source is found online, and it doesn't fit into any other category, then it gets classified as a website or web page.

Website with a group author
A consideration when using websites as sources is whether they would be considered to be "legitimate." There are times when a website may provide you with the most up-to-date information on a particular topic or a definition that you cannot find elsewhere. Information from sources like the Centers for Disease Control (cdc.gov), the National Institute of Mental Health (nimh.nih.gov), and the Mayo Clinic (mayoclinic.org) are credible, legitimate, and cover a variety of scientific topics.

The information from these sources usually comes from a "group author," meaning the organization itself. In the first two examples below, the "author" is the organization, the date is the most recent update to the page (NOT the day you accessed the information), the title of the information is in italics, and the URL of the web page is provided.

Centers for Disease Control and Prevention. (2017, September 6). *Stroke facts.*
http://www.cdc.gov/stroke/facts

National Institute of Mental Health. (2019, May). *Post-Traumatic Stress Disorder (PTSD).*
http://www.nimh.nih.gov/health/topics/post-traumatic-stress-disorder-ptsd/index.shtml

Sometimes sites will list an author, such as "Mayo Clinic Staff." In these cases, use that as the "author" (Mayo Clinic Staff) and include the organization they are a part of (Mayo Clinic) in the reference. Otherwise, the retrieval information is the same, and would look like:

Mayo Clinic Staff. (2017, October 25). *Seasonal affective disorder (SAD).* Mayo Clinic.
https://www.mayoclinic.org/diseases-conditions/seasonal-affective-disorder/symptoms-causes/syc-20364651

Mayo Clinic Staff. (2019, June 1). *Diseases and conditions: Stroke.* Mayo Clinic.
http://www.mayoclinic.org/diseases-conditions/stroke/basics/definition/con-20042884

Website with an individual author
The problem with websites is that unlike research journals, they are not peer-reviewed, so any author can pretty much write anything, and who knows if it has any validity? However, many students will use information from websites to provide examples and anecdotes for their paper.

The reference follows the same basic pattern as the previous examples - author, date, title of the material (in italics), source (or "publisher") of the material, and retrieval information (the URL). Examples follow:

McIntosh, J. (2014, September 5). *What is stroke? What causes strokes?* Medical News Today. http://www.medicalnewstoday.com/articles/7624.php#treatment_and_prevention

Paddock, M., & Nordqvist, C. (2014, September 26). *What is claustrophobia? What causes claustrophobia?* Medical News Today. http://www.medicalnewstoday.com/articles/37062.php

Sher, D. (2018, October 27). *Claustrophobia and anxiety: Causes and solutions.* Calm Clinic. http://www.calmclinic.com/anxiety/symptoms/claustrophobia

The news website

Who reads a physical newspaper anymore? Many people get their news from the web, and the same basic format works for any "news" website you choose. Examples follow:

Brunner, J. (2014, March 4). *On the 110th anniversary of Dr. Seuss's birth his quotes continue to inspire.* HuffPost. http://www.huffingtonpost.com/jeryl-brunner/on-the-100th-anniversary-_b_4891306.html

Strickland, A. (2020, January 24). *Some Mount Vesuvius victims suffered slowly and one victim's brain turned to glass, new research says.* CNN. https://www.cnn.com/2020/01/23/world/mount-vesuvius-herculaneum-skeletons-scn/index.html

The website with no date

APA style makes it clear that if there is no identifiable date on a web page, using "n.d." for "no date" is acceptable. The following example is set up like the "group author" examples above, except for the "date" information:

Duke General Psychiatry Division. (n.d.). *Virtual reality therapy for phobias.* http://psychiatry.duke.edu/divisions/general-psychiatry/virtual-reality-therapy-phobias

Reference management software - all your problems solved?

There's a technological solution for every problem, and the same is true for citation and reference. I would feel remiss if I closed this section without discussing reference management software programs like Zotero, RefWorks, Mendeley, and about 20 others! Basically, after you scale the learning curve of how to use them, they correctly construct your citations and references in whatever format you choose - APA, MLA, Vancouver, Bratislavan, Chicago, and any other system in their database. So what's not to love? The learning curve.

If you're writing a few APA style papers on different topics over the course of your college career, I don't think that reference management software is worth the time. It's the equivalent of bringing a howitzer to kill a housefly. If you're a professor or graduate student writing multiple articles on the same topic for years though, it's the best thing since sliced bread, mostly because it organizes the hundreds (if not thousands) of sources you're likely to use over your academic writing career.

Odds and ends

Fonts and formatting

APA style requires writers to use only a few approved fonts. For example, 11-point Calibri, Arial, or Georgia, 10-point Lucinda Sans Unicode, or 12-point Times New Roman are all acceptable in the body of a paper. This might seem obvious, but you should pick a font and stick with it throughout the paper; DON'T change fonts between sections, paragraphs, etc. If you include figures in your manuscript, any of the above fonts are acceptable as long as the type remains between 8 and 14 points.

APA style requires that papers are double-spaced with 1 inch (2.54 cm) margins all around (top, bottom, left, right) the manuscript. The sample student paper and journal submission both follow this format.

Although many books on APA style include a section (often running to 20-30 pages) on how to use Microsoft Word or Google Docs to set up an APA style paper, I think this is a topic where "showing" through an instructional video is much better than trying to learn from screen shots inserted into a book. However, if you would like more guidance on how to use a word processing program, a very simple solution is to google "APA style google doc" or "APA style MS Word" and you will immediately be presented with a number of templates and "fill-in-the-blank" sample papers, many of which are very good! The templates are usually distributed by educators who care about writing.

Bias-free writing

Part of writing clearly involves using specific, acceptable, and appropriate terms for the people who participate in research. For example, when writing about older adults, "older persons" and "persons 65 years and older" are appropriate, where "the elderly" or "seniors" are not. Similarly, the terms "child," "girl," and "boy" (and more specifically, "transgender girl" or "gender-fluid child") are appropriate when referring to people under 12 years old, and "young woman" or "young man" (or "female adolescent," "agender adolescent," etc.) are appropriate for people between the ages of 13 and 17.

Terms for sexual orientation should be specific and sensitive, and so "lesbians," "gay men," "straight," "queer," etc. are acceptable. I would note that "sexual orientation" is the proper term, rather than "sexual preference" or "sexual identity."

Terms for racial and ethnic identity follow the same logic of being specific and appropriate. In general, be as specific as you need to be, so if you are studying people in Cuba, it is appropriate to refer to them as Cubans. If you are studying people from Cuba who are living in the United States, they are Cuban Americans (no hyphen). "Blacks" and "Whites" are considered proper nouns and are capitalized. Census categories of people are considered to be appropriate for APA style.

Finally, in terms of pronouns, APA style endorses the use of the singular "they" as a generic third-person singular pronoun. For years, the use of the singular "they" was discouraged in academic writing as being non-specific, but in the last decade many publishers have embraced the term, and so now it is part of APA style.

A note on plagiarism

The detection of plagiarism in student papers has gotten vastly easier over the past decade with the introduction of online tools such as TurnItIn.com and SafeAssign. Both of these tools compare a paper not just to every journal article in their databases, but to every website, and every other paper ever submitted to the service. This means that you could get flagged for rewriting one of your OWN papers that you had turned in for another class.

However, most professors don't need a program to detect plagiarism. The "voice" of the paper just changes, or students begin using words and phrases that make it clear that they're copying down someone else's words or ideas. Students oftentimes don't understand that they've plagiarized if they've included a citation.

So how do you know when you've stepped over a line? Perhaps you're familiar with the "general rule" that's out there that if you use five identical words in a row without a direct quote citation, you've plagiarized. Well, maybe. It's not that difficult to paraphrase the writing of others; it just requires a little effort.

Let's take a look at an actual student paper on conformity. This was a "D" paper because it had numerous other issues (like the student misspelling the author they were plagiarizing). We can start out with the source they used, and then compare that to what the student wrote - the words that are plagiarized are in bold.

Source:

Natarajan, R. C. (2009). Halo effect in trust. *IUP Journal of Management Research, 8*(1), 26-59.

What the student wrote:

A study by RC Natarjan demonstrates about how a **principal may trust an agent due to either the latter's ability to carry out the task as competence trust** or to the perception **that the latter will not act in a manner detrimental to the relationship or the former (goodwill trust)**.

Natarajan (2009) source:

A principal may trust an agent either due to the latter's ability to carry out the task as desired (competence trust) or due to the perception that the latter will not act in a manner detrimental to the relationship of the former (goodwill trust).

A few comments. First, be sure to correctly spell the names of the authors you are plagiarizing. Second, in a 50 word sentence, 40 of the words are "identical words in a row" without a direct quote citation. While I would admit that the source material is not the clearest writing, a corrected, non-plagiarizing paraphrasing of the same source would read as follows:

A study by Natarajan (2009) demonstrates how a person might trust another person by either their ability to complete a task (called "competence trust") or their actions in building a relationship (called "goodwill trust").

The author is cited correctly (without including their first and middle name initials) and the sentence has been put through the "de-jargoning machine" to distill the essence of what the researcher is trying to say, while also including the critical terms they discuss.

Here's another example from the same paper, again with the words that are the same in bold:

According to Natarjan, **competence trust is formed through the principal's awareness and conviction regarding the agent's skills, financial ability and consistency in performance.**

Natarajan (2009) source:

For example, competence trust is formed through the principal's awareness and conviction regarding the agent's skills, financial ability and consistency in performance - thus providing reliability.

If anything, this is an even more egregious example because in a 23 word sentence, 20 of the words are "identical words in a row." The student didn't even correct for the improper lack of an Oxford (or serial) comma after the word "ability!"

Correction:

According to Natarajan (2009), competence trust is created through "the principal's awareness and conviction regarding the agent's skills, financial ability and consistency in performance" (p. 50).

In this case, a direct quote is appropriate because there's no really good way to paraphrase this sentence. As always, quotations should be used sparingly, but too many properly cited quotes is better than outright plagiarism.

I hope this section has made it evident that while often inadvertent, plagiarism is easily avoided by taking the time and effort to paraphrase a source or by simply using a direct quotation.

Quotations - Direct and block

Sometimes we need to use a direct quote in a paper in order to get the wording exactly right; however, I strongly discourage my students from using direct quotes very frequently. Like block quotes (to be discussed momentarily), direct quotes can be used to pad out the length of a paper, and that can be pretty obvious to a professor. Some papers I've read are really just strings of direct quotes bound together with some intervening explanatory sentences. There have also been a number of times I've scratched my head and asked, "Why did they need to take a direct quote of THAT?!" Nothing shows an inability to paraphrase like the overuse of direct quotes.

Whenever you use a direct quotation from one of your sources, be sure to always specify an author, year, and page (or paragraph, in the case of websites and some other media) in the citation of the quotation. Direct quotations are only appropriate if they are 40 words or less. If they're more than 40 words, they should be incorporated into a block quotation (and indented ½ inch from the left margin).

A direct quotation must faithfully reproduce the spelling, wording, and punctuation of the original source material, so you can't edit or change it. If there is a particular word (or words) that you want to emphasize within the quotation, put them into italics followed by [emphasis added] in brackets. Also, if your direct quotation contains a citation, include it in the quotation (after all, you're "faithfully reproducing" the original source), but don't add it to your reference list: you're not using it as a source, the other author of the quotation is. If you're taking a direct quote from an online source that doesn't have page numbers (and not many do), use the paragraph number that the quote appears in, and use the abbreviation "para." in your citation.

Numbers and percentages

One might say that there are a number of rules for writing about numbers. In general, numerals (e.g. 11, 51, 136) should be used to express numbers starting with the number 10 (and higher). However, there are a number of exceptions to this! For example, words should be used to indicate numbers when a number begins a sentence, a text heading, or a title. Words should also be used to indicate numbers less than 10 (which logically follows if you're using numerals for numbers 10 and higher). When you're dealing with decimal fractions (like 0.012 or 0.15), a zero should be placed before the decimal point only in cases where the statistic (such as a t value or F value) can be greater than one. If the decimal fraction cannot be greater than one (like in a p value), there's no need to include a zero (e.g., $p < .001, p = .012$).

Numerals should also be used to represent units of time, dates, ages, points on a scale, and exact units of money.

Okay, so that's numbers, but what about percentages? Those are numbers, right? Actually, the same rules apply! Sort of. According to APA style, you should use the "%" symbol when it is preceded by a numeral, which it almost always is, so you would write "5%" even though "5" is a number less than 10 (and so would usually be written out as a word). You should use the word "percent" or "percentage" when it is preceded by a word (so, for example, at the beginning of a sentence).

So, you would write "23%" rather than "twenty-three percent" or "23 percent" and "8%" rather than "eight percent" or "eight %" (personally, my favorite permutation - the word WITH the symbol).

Sample student paper

It's one thing to understand the rules of APA style, and another to apply them in an actual paper. Therefore, this section includes an annotated student paper from my Experimental Psychology class. The student who wrote it later became one of my teaching assistants, and the paper is reproduced with their permission.

I've included "comment bubbles" throughout the paper, but wanted to point out a few things.

1. While the paper includes an abstract, this is not required in an APA style student paper unless the professor requests one. I requested one.

2. The paper includes sources from websites and TED Talks. These should be used sparingly!

3. The paper includes great examples of how to incorporate direct quotes into a manuscript, including when you have to cut material (and use an ellipsis to show where the cut was made) or insert explanatory information (with [brackets]).

4. Throughout the paper, there are examples of how to properly write about numbers - when you should use numerals and when you should spell them out (like at the beginning of a sentence).

5. Throughout the paper are examples of how to properly cite sources with one, two, and three or more authors.

6. The reference list contains a good example of how to alphabetize when you have two sources by the same author (HINT: You alphabetize by the last name of the second author!).

7. If you would like to see the manuscript without all the "comment bubbles," I have put a "clean" version of it up on my APACentral.com website!

29

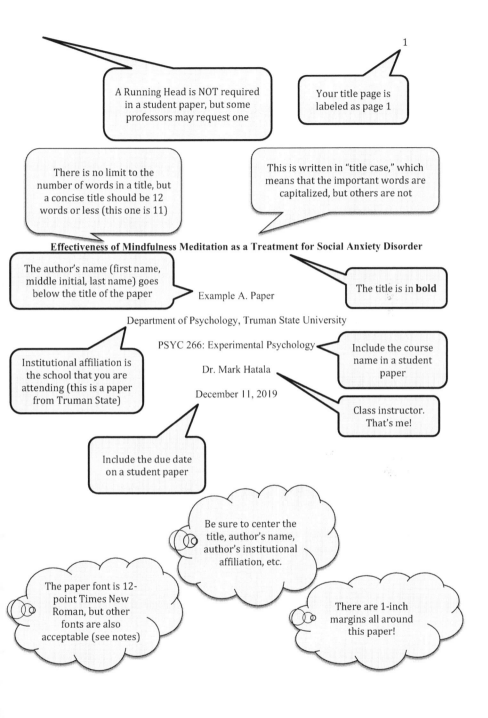

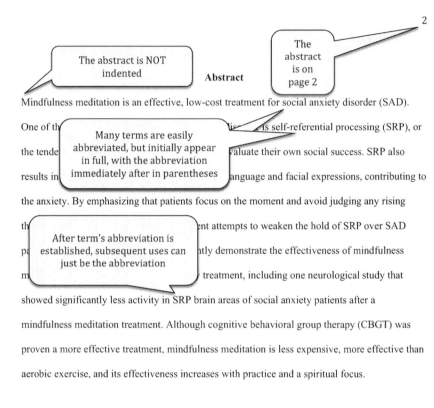

Abstract

Mindfulness meditation is an effective, low-cost treatment for social anxiety disorder (SAD). One of th[...]is self-referential processing (SRP), or the tende[...]valuate their own social success. SRP also results in[...]anguage and facial expressions, contributing to the anxiety. By emphasizing that patients focus on the moment and avoid judging any rising th[...]nt attempts to weaken the hold of SRP over SAD p[...]tly demonstrate the effectiveness of mindfulness m[...]treatment, including one neurological study that showed significantly less activity in SRP brain areas of social anxiety patients after a mindfulness meditation treatment. Although cognitive behavioral group therapy (CBGT) was proven a more effective treatment, mindfulness meditation is less expensive, more effective than aerobic exercise, and its effectiveness increases with practice and a spiritual focus.

Keywords: mindfulness meditation, social anxiety disorder, self-referential processing

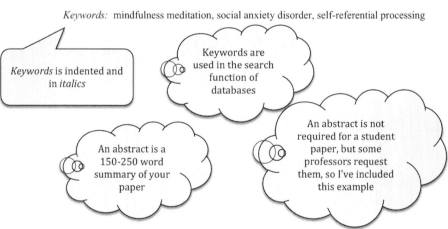

3

Effectiveness of Mindfulness Meditation as a Treatment for Social Anxiety Disorder

The teenage boy stumbles into a bathroom stall. He is ☐ school, but his teary eyes, sweaty brow, and quickened breath suggest some great trau ☐ as pushed him over the edge. His ☐ won again. From drugs to ☐ he has tried everything to def ☐ can abate the rush of ☐ high schoo ☐ every day. They only reflect what he ☐ himself:

judgment. That one word summarizes the daily internal war those afflicted with social anxiety disorder (SAD), like the teenage boy, endure. Social anxiety disorder is an intense, persistent phobia of social situations (Goldin et al., 2009), due ☐ in social settings (Goldin et al., 2013). One potential treatme ☐ meditation. ☐ ttention for a period of time without evaluating any rising thoughts (☐ the meditation could combat distorted self-judgment during social interactions, a key symptom of social anxiety. This paper evaluates the effectiveness of mindfulness meditation in treating social anxiety, compares the treatment to other treatments for social anxiety, and explores ways to improve the effectiveness of the treatment.

By learning how ☐ owledge perceptions without an ☐ meditation can help s ☐ ally anxious individuals gain control over ☐ self-evaluation in social situations (TED, 2014). According to Edenfield and Saeed's (2012) review of mindfulness meditatio ☐ er self-judgment encourages patients to socialize without as much dis ☐ and avoidance behaviors feeding the anxiety. As a treatment ☐ al. (2013) reported that mindfulness meditation has been successfu ☐ "improved mood, functionality and quality of life in patients with SAD" (p. 244). Additionally, Edenfield and Saeed (2012) said in their review of mindfulness meditation

Callouts: Begin a paper with a "hook" to draw the reader in | The title is centered, in **bold,** and in title case | The body of the paper begins on page 3 | A citation with three authors lists just the first author followed by "et al." | The introduction concludes with a thesis statement | This is a TED talk on YouTube | A citation with two authors lists both authors every time | A direct quotation contains the page # where it appears in the original source

research that one meta-analysis reported the treatment h[...] than a

placebo treatment.

Goldin et al. (2009) attempted to discover neurological changes in patients with social

anxiety after [...] recruiting 16 participants through the

web and loca[...] patients were given a questionnaire about

their mental state, [...] SRT task. Since few subjects were available and the

experiment[...] were interested in a more specific condition and treatment, they performed a

small-N AB experiment, measuring patients' baseline social anxiety before mindfulness

meditation and measuring it again afterwards. During the fMRI participants were flashed with a

que[...] [posi]tive social trait. They [...]

ans[...] [posi]tive or negative, capita[...]

dep[...] patients were evaluating [...]

negatively, the midline c[...] brain regions and language proc[...] areas, or regions related to

self-evaluation, lit up. Goldin et al. (2009) claimed this demonstrated those with SAD

"automatically rely on a … self-focus that recruits [internal dialogue] brain systems" (p. 250) or

rather, that the unhealthy self-evaluation of SAD patients is focused in those areas.

Patients then participated in eight weekly 2.5-hour sessions of mindfulness meditation, a

ha[...] after session 6, and daily [h]ome practice. Experimenters monitored

ev[...] [pra]ctices daily. A[...] the [treat]ment, when asked to self-report their

mental state again, the treatment "resulted in mo[...] [reduc]tion of symptoms of social anxiety,

depression, rumination, and state anxiety and increas[...] [est]eem" (Goldin et al., 2009, p. 252).

At the end of 8 weeks of mindfulness meditation [...] to

themselves during the fMRI. Self-evaluation bra[...]

effectiveness of mindfulness meditation in reduc[...]

Callout annotations:

Numerals should be used to express numbers 10 and above

The "N" in "small-N" is not italicized because it is referring to a type of design rather than the total number of people in a sample

If you cut material from a direct quotation, use ellipses (…) to show where the cut was made

Use [brackets] to insert explanatory information into a direct quote

Results are discussed in the past tense

Numerals rather than words should be used to express specific time, dates, and experimental procedures for numbers 10 and below

5

Despite mindfulness meditation's potential success as a SAD treatment, other treatments

may lead to better results. In an experiment done by Koszyci et al. (2007), 53 SAD patients were

randomly assigned to either 8 weeks of mindfulness meditation or 12 weekly sessions of CBGT.

Koszyci et al. (2007) f⋯⋯⋯⋯nts receiving CBGT had significantly lower social anxiety

s⋯⋯⋯⋯⋯⋯⋯⋯⋯⋯ission rates were significantly greater for the CBGT group.

H⋯⋯⋯⋯⋯patients with generalized SAD in a randomized controlled

> A citation with four authors lists just the first author followed by "et al."

trial were randomly assigned to 8 weeks of mindfulness meditation or 8 weeks of an aerobic

exercise program (Goldin et al., 2013). An fMRI and a self-report clinical and well-being

measure were given to every s⋯⋯ before and after the treatment (Goldin et. al, 2013). At the

end of t⋯⋯⋯⋯⋯⋯⋯⋯⋯ower self-reported social anxiety

sympto⋯⋯⋯⋯⋯⋯⋯on-regulating parietal cortical regions' neural

respons⋯⋯⋯⋯⋯⋯⋯⋯⋯⋯⋯ments (Goldin et. al, 2013). Thus,

mindfulnes⋯⋯ation proved more effective than aerobic exe⋯⋯⋯⋯ et

al., 2013). Although CGBT proved more effective than mindful⋯⋯⋯⋯⋯s

meditation could be a viable low-cost alternative to CBGT (Vaynerman, 2017).

> The problem with using a parenthetical citation is that the same article needs to be re-cited every time it is paraphrased

> Use websites as sources sparingly

Additionally, there are potential ways to compensate for mindfulness meditation's lower

ef⋯⋯⋯⋯⋯⋯⋯ccording to Edenfi⋯⋯⋯⋯re

ex⋯⋯⋯⋯⋯⋯⋯ffective meditation⋯⋯⋯⋯ to

m⋯⋯⋯⋯⋯⋯⋯or SAD, practice could⋯⋯⋯⋯erfect. One experiment

found that the effectiveness⋯⋯meditation depended heavily on whether or not the meditation had a

religious context (Wachholtz & Pargament, 2005). Eighty-four college students were recruited for

th⋯⋯⋯⋯⋯⋯⋯ants in a Spiritual Meditation group, 21 participants in a Secular

M⋯⋯⋯⋯⋯⋯⋯⋯⋯⋯ with 22 participants (Wachholtz &

Pargament, 2005). All participants practiced their technique in isolation 20 minutes a day for 2

> For a source with two authors, both authors should be cited every time the source is cited

> Numbers should be spelled out when they begin a sentence

> Numerals should be used to express numbers 10 and above

weeks (Wachholtz & Pargament, 2005). However, the spiritual group said phrases with a religious

focus as they meditated l̶̶̶̶̶ ̶̶̶̶is good," the secular group said positive phrases like "I am

goo̶

200̶

low̶ ̶̶̶̶̶̶̶̶̶̶t. Thus, a spiritual focus and meditation experience could

> For a source with two authors, both authors should be cited every time the source is cited

̶̶̶̶̶̶̶̶s (Wachholtz & Pargament,

o meditate with a religious focus showed significantly

improve mindfulness meditation results for SAD patients.

In conclusion, mindfulness meditation could provide an excellent, low-cost alternative to

other SAD therapies. Although CBGT has been p̶̶̶̶̶̶̶̶̶ ̶̶̶̶̶ore effective as a SAD treatment,

mindfulness can reduce anxiety and SRP. Ad̶ experience,

mindfulness meditation's effectiveness can i ̶̶̶̶̶̶̶ay not be

> The conclusion is the place to insert your own perspective, as long as it is framed properly

completely valid when issues with the experiments cited are taken into account. As an AB

experiment, Goldin et al.'s (2009) neurological study does not have high internal validity.

Internal validity could be increased by ̶̶̶̶̶̶ng the subjects after several weeks without any

̶̶̶̶̶̶ a return to baseline conditions. Since it would be

̶̶̶̶̶̶ients untreated, mindfulness meditation sessions would

̶̶̶̶̶he new basel̶̶̶̶̶ ̶̶̶̶̶̶̶̶̶. Additionally, Wachholtz and

> The conclusion is also the appropriate place to point out the shortcomings of the research reviewed

Pargament's (2005) experiment on religious medit̶ ̶̶̶̶̶s

specifically on social anxiety. Although a spiritual ̶̶̶̶̶s

> The conclusion should also be used to discuss possible future areas of research

effectiveness for generalized anxiety, a religious f̶̶̶̶̶̶̶̶̶̶ight not improve meditation's impact on

social anxiety. In general, more research pertaining to SAD and mindfulness meditation could be

useful to truly determine the reliability of a connection between the two, as most research only

explores mindfulness meditation and generalized anxiety.

7

References

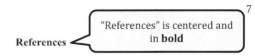

"References" is centered and in **bold**

Edenfield T. M., & Saeed S., A. (2012). An update on mindfulness meditation as a self-help

 treatment for anxiety and depression. *Psychology Research & Behavior Management, 5,*

 131-141. http://doi.org/10.2147/PRBM.S34937

Goldin, P., Ramel, W., & Gross, J. (2009). Mindfulness meditation training and self-referential

 processing in social anxiety disorder: Ben... ...gnitive

 Psychotherapy, 23(3), 242-...

When you have two sources by the same author, alphabetize by the last name of the second author

Goldin, P., Ziv, M., Jazaieri, H., Hahn, K., & Gross, J. J. (2013). MBSR vs. aerobic exercise in

 social anxiety: fMRI of emotion regulation of negative self-beliefs. *Social Cognitive &*

 Affective Neuroscience, 8(1), 65-72. http://doi.org/10.1093/scan/nss054

Koszycki, D., Benger, M., Shlik, J., & Bradwejn, J. (2007). Randomized trial of a meditation-

 based stress reduction program and... ...ial

 anxiety disorder. *Behaviour Resear*...

A TED talk available on YouTube

TED. (2014, November 24). *Kasim Al-Mashat:* ...*mindfulness meditation redefines pain,*

 happiness, and satisfaction [Video]. YouTube. https://www.youtube.com/

 watch?v=JVwLJc5etEQ

Vaynerman, S. (2017, December 6). *Thr*... ...*tion techniques to practice at*

A news website

 home or at the office. HuffPost. https://www.huffpost.com/entry/three-easy-mindfullness

Wachholtz, A. B., & Pargament, K. I. (2005). Is spirituality a critical ingredient of meditation?

 Comparing the effects of spiritual meditation, secular meditation, and relaxation on

 spiritual, psy... ...ical, cardiac, and pain outcomes. *Journal of Behavioral Medicine,*

 28(4), 369-... ...5-005-9008-5

All lines in a reference after the first line are indented ½ inch

Sample professional paper

The sample professional paper is a journal submission that I've been unsuccessfully trying to get published for several years. It fills a very small niche in the literature on memory and the recall of odors, but apparently the niche is so small that journal editors have not been able to see it! This manuscript is something of a "one-off" anyway, as it does not really fit in with the rest of my research program.

To save space, I've chosen not to reprint the entire manuscript, but rather the "significant" pages (the main sections and Level 1 headers). This manuscript is far from perfect (it is, after all, unpublished), but it is a reasonable example of a professional paper or journal submission.

As with the example student paper, I've included "comment bubbles" throughout the paper, but wanted to point out a few things.

1. A Running Head appears at the top of every page because this is a professional paper. The purpose of a Running Head? Who knows?

2. The paper includes sources from websites and *Wikipedia*. I would never actually use *Wikipedia* as a source in a journal submission, but I thought it would be good to show the citation and reference in the context of a paper.

3. Throughout the paper, there are examples of how to properly write about numbers - when you should use numerals and when you should spell them out (like at the beginning of a sentence).

4. The paper contains examples of how to write about an Appendix and Tables.

5. The reference list includes journal articles with shortened DOI numbers (from the website shortdoi.org) as well as journal articles with long-form DOI numbers. BOTH are acceptable in a student or professional paper.

6. The reference list contains a good example of how to alphabetize when you have two sources by the same author (HINT: "Nothing" comes before something!).

7. If you would like to see the manuscript without all the "comment bubbles," I have put a "clean" version of it up on my APACentral.com website!

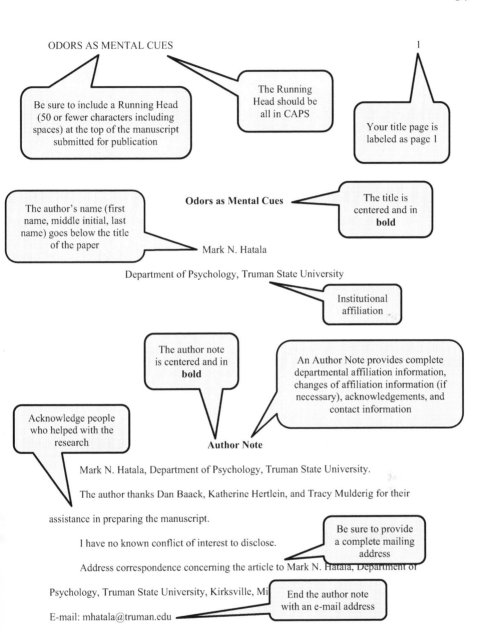

38

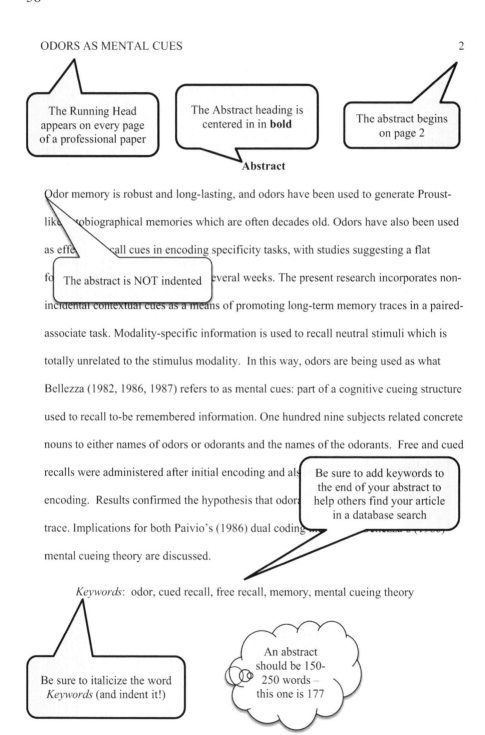

Abstract

Odor memory is robust and long-lasting, and odors have been used to generate Proust-like autobiographical memories which are often decades old. Odors have also been used as effective recall cues in encoding specificity tasks, with studies suggesting a flat forgetting curve over several weeks. The present research incorporates non-incidental contextual cues as a means of promoting long-term memory traces in a paired-associate task. Modality-specific information is used to recall neutral stimuli which is totally unrelated to the stimulus modality. In this way, odors are being used as what Bellezza (1982, 1986, 1987) refers to as mental cues: part of a cognitive cueing structure used to recall to-be remembered information. One hundred nine subjects related concrete nouns to either names of odors or odorants and the names of the odorants. Free and cued recalls were administered after initial encoding and also encoding. Results confirmed the hypothesis that odors trace. Implications for both Paivio's (1986) dual coding and Bellezza's (1986) mental cueing theory are discussed.

Keywords: odor, cued recall, free recall, memory, mental cueing theory

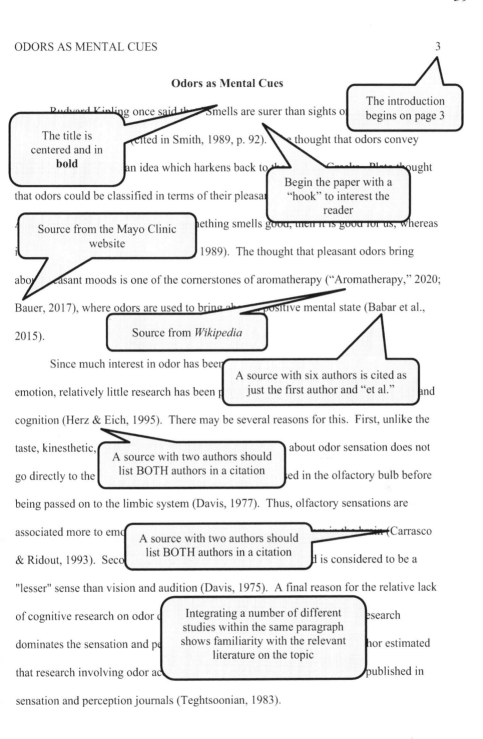

Odors as Mental Cues

Rudyard Kipling once said that "Smells are surer than sights o[r] ... (cited in Smith, 1989, p. 92). ...e thought that odors convey an idea which harkens back to the ... Greeks. Plato thought that odors could be classified in terms of their pleasa... ...nething smells good, then it is good for us, whereas i... 1989). The thought that pleasant odors bring abo... ...easant moods is one of the cornerstones of aromatherapy ("Aromatherapy," 2020; Bauer, 2017), where odors are used to bring ab... ...positive mental state (Babar et al., 2015).

Since much interest in odor has been ... emotion, relatively little research has been p... ...and cognition (Herz & Eich, 1995). There may be several reasons for this. First, unlike the taste, kinesthetic, ... about odor sensation does not go directly to the ...ed in the olfactory bulb before being passed on to the limbic system (Davis, 1977). Thus, olfactory sensations are associated more to emo... ...in the brain (Carrasco & Ridout, 1993). Seco... ...d is considered to be a "lesser" sense than vision and audition (Davis, 1975). A final reason for the relative lack of cognitive research on odor ... ...search dominates the sensation and p... ...hor estimated that research involving odor ac... ...published in sensation and perception journals (Teghtsoonian, 1983).

Callout annotations:

- The introduction begins on page 3
- The title is centered and in **bold**
- Begin the paper with a "hook" to interest the reader
- Source from the Mayo Clinic website
- Source from *Wikipedia*
- A source with six authors is cited as just the first author and "et al."
- A source with two authors should list BOTH authors in a citation
- A source with two authors should list BOTH authors in a citation
- Integrating a number of different studies within the same paragraph shows familiarity with the relevant literature on the topic

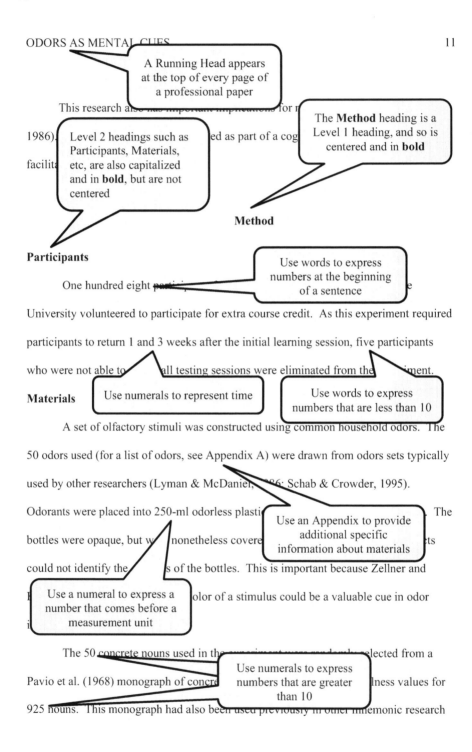

cued or free recall of the list words. In the cued recall, [*Use numerals to express numbers that are greater than 10*] go

from table to table looking at the names of the odors, wh[...] in the free recall they had

to just try to remember the names of the 50 odors. Participants were then debriefed and

dismissed.

Participants were invited back for a cued or free recall (depending on which they

had performed at the initial encoding session) both 1 week and 3 weeks after the initial

encoding session. Again, for the cued [*Use numerals for numbers that represent time*] go around to all of

the tables and smell the odorants or lo[...] [...]roup that they were

in). Participants in the free recall con[...] just sat and reca[...] [*The **Results** heading is a Level 1 heading and is centered and in **bold***]

words as they could for 8 minutes.

Results

List word recall for the first experimental session was examined with a 2 x 2

(Odor [odorants and odor names, odor names] x Recall [cued, free]) analysis of variance

[*In a factorial design, in parentheses list the independent variables, and in brackets, the treatment levels for each independent variable*] [...]ffect for the recall condition, $F(1, 104) =$

[...] for the use of [*Provide the obtained value of the statistic, the degrees of freedom, the p-value, and the effect size*]

[...]ts who were g[...]

[...]recall session were able to recall far more words than p[...]

perform just a free recall. This can be seen clearly in Table 1 below. These [...]ts,

however, must be interpreted in light of a signifi[...] [...]y interaction, $F(1, 104) = 5.33$,

$p < .02$, $\eta_p^2 = .04$. [*Tables are pointed out in the text*]

Results for familiarity and pleasantness ratings were mixed. When looking at

familiarity ratings of all 50 odors, there were no effects for odor or recall condition;

however, when examining the pleasantness ratings, participants who received both the

42

odor and odor name rated the odors as being less pleasant than subjects who just received

the odor names, $F(1, 104) = 8.06$, $p < .005$, , $\eta_p^2 = .15$. This suggests that while familiarity

is unaffected by memory, subjects have more p...ey

are ac... s.

...iarity and pleasantness ratings for words which

were an... ...e not recalled showed no differences betw...

Table 2.

> Be sure to clearly identify Tables by number

> Provide the obtained value of the statistic, the degrees of freedom, the *p*-value, and the effect size

> The **Discussion** heading is a Level 1 heading and is centered and in **bold**

Discussion

Results confirmed the hypothesis that initial recall would have a strong main

effect for recall condition, with cued recall outperforming free recall. There was no

difference between groups as ...whether they received odors at encoding or not. This

seems logical and was predicted be... ...lthough participants who get both the odor

name and the odor may have bet... ...who did not receive the

olfactory stimuli had more time... ...lthough there was a

significant interaction, it was mos... ...ain effect for recall

condition. The omega squared value for the recall c... ...while

the omega squared value for the interaction is .041. ...ll,

odor plays a negligible role in the recall process.

> The Discussion should "discuss" whether experimental hypotheses were supported

> Interpret results in the present tense in order to bring the reader into the "discussion"

The pleasantness ratings of the odors are interesting because participants who

actually received the odors rated them as less pleasant than participants who did not

receive the odors. Perhaps memories for common household odors are stored as some

sort of abstract, idealized prototype, so that the actual odor when presented is not as

pleasant as we remember.

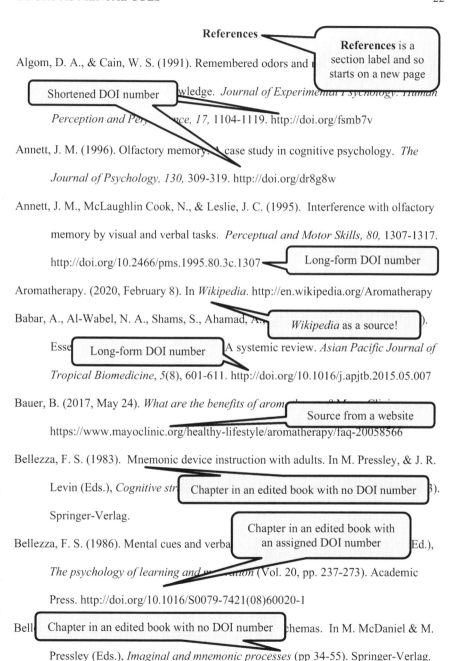

References

References is a section label and so starts on a new page

Algom, D. A., & Cain, W. S. (1991). Remembered odors and ... wledge. *Journal of Experimental Psychology: Human Perception and Per...nce, 17,* 1104-1119. http://doi.org/fsmb7v

Shortened DOI number

Annett, J. M. (1996). Olfactory memory: A case study in cognitive psychology. *The Journal of Psychology, 130,* 309-319. http://doi.org/dr8g8w

Annett, J. M., McLaughlin Cook, N., & Leslie, J. C. (1995). Interference with olfactory memory by visual and verbal tasks. *Perceptual and Motor Skills, 80,* 1307-1317. http://doi.org/10.2466/pms.1995.80.3c.1307

Long-form DOI number

Aromatherapy. (2020, February 8). In *Wikipedia.* http://en.wikipedia.org/Aromatherapy

Wikipedia as a source!

Babar, A., Al-Wabel, N. A., Shams, S., Ahamad, A...). Esse... A systemic review. *Asian Pacific Journal of Tropical Biomedicine, 5*(8), 601-611. http://doi.org/10.1016/j.apjtb.2015.05.007

Long-form DOI number

Bauer, B. (2017, May 24). *What are the benefits of arom...* https://www.mayoclinic.org/healthy-lifestyle/aromatherapy/faq-20058566

Source from a website

Bellezza, F. S. (1983). Mnemonic device instruction with adults. In M. Pressley, & J. R. Levin (Eds.), *Cognitive str...* ...). Springer-Verlag.

Chapter in an edited book with no DOI number

Bellezza, F. S. (1986). Mental cues and verba... ...Ed.), *The psychology of learning and ...ation* (Vol. 20, pp. 237-273). Academic Press. http://doi.org/10.1016/S0079-7421(08)60020-1

Chapter in an edited book with an assigned DOI number

Bell... ...hemas. In M. McDaniel & M. Pressley (Eds.), *Imaginal and mnemonic processes* (pp 34-55). Springer-Verlag.

Chapter in an edited book with no DOI number

Made in the USA
Coppell, TX
27 September 2020

38869137R00024